WHAT WE STAND FOR

LAND OF THE FREE

the kids' book of
FREEDOM

ANDERS HANSON

CONSULTING EDITOR, DIANE CRAIG, M.A./READING SPECIALIST

Super Sandcastle

An Imprint of Abdo Publishing
www.abdopublishing.com

visit us at www.abdopublishing.com

Published by Abdo Publishing, a division of ABDO, PO Box 398166, Minneapolis, Minnesota 55439.
Copyright © 2015 by Abdo Consulting Group, Inc. International copyrights reserved in all countries.
No part of this book may be reproduced in any form without written permission from the publisher.
Super SandCastle™ is a trademark and logo of Abdo Publishing.

Printed in the United States of America, North Mankato, Minnesota
062014
092014

Editor: Liz Salzmann
Content Developer: Nancy Tuminelly
Cover and Interior Design and Production: Anders Hanson, Mighty Media, Inc.
Photo Credits: Shutterstock

Library of Congress Cataloging-in-Publication Data

Hanson, Anders, 1980-
  Land of the free : the kids' book of freedom / Anders Hanson, Consulting Editor, Diane Craig, M.A.,
Reading Specialist.
      pages cm. -- (What we stand for)
  ISBN 978-1-62403-295-0
1. Liberty--United States--Juvenile literature. 2. Democracy--United States--Juvenile literature.
3. Civil rights--United States--Juvenile literature. I. Title.
  JC599.U5H265 2015
  323.440973--dc23
                        2013041841

Super SandCastle™ books are created by a team of professional educators, reading specialists, and
content developers around five essential components—phonemic awareness, phonics, vocabulary, text
comprehension, and fluency—to assist young readers as they develop reading skills and strategies and
increase their general knowledge. All books are written, reviewed, and leveled for guided reading, early
reading intervention, and Accelerated Reader® programs for use in shared, guided, and independent
reading and writing activities to support a balanced approach to literacy instruction.

CONTENTS

WHAT IS
FREEDOM?

Freedom means having the right to make choices about your life.

It's the 4th of July. Maya waves a small American flag.

The United
States has many
freedoms.

Mark and his
four friends
stand on a hill.
They hold a huge
American flag.

In the United States, many freedoms are **protected** by the bill of rights.

The Bill of Rights is part of the **constitution**.

The **United Nations** lists rights for children. It's called the Declaration of the Rights of the Child.

It is for all children in the world. It says children have the right to life, health care, and education.

HOW ARE YOU
FREE?

What are your freedoms?

FREEDOM
TO VOTE

Adults have the freedom to vote.

Voters decide who the leaders will be.

FREEDOM OF RELIGION

Freedom of **religion** means you have the right to believe in any religion. So does everyone else.

FREEDOM TO CHOOSE WHERE TO LIVE

Adults have the right to choose where to live. They can live anywhere.

Tim and Carson's parents chose to live in Minnesota. They moved there from Iowa.

FREEDOM OF SPEECH

You have the right
to your own ideas.
You can tell people
what you think.

FREEDOM TO GO TO SCHOOL

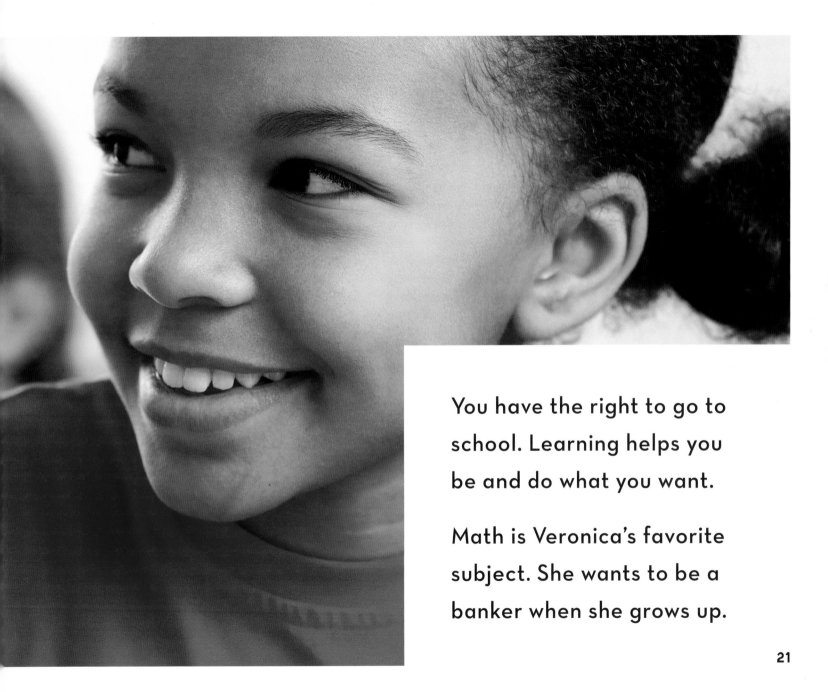

You have the right to go to school. Learning helps you be and do what you want.

Math is Veronica's favorite subject. She wants to be a banker when she grows up.

WHAT WILL YOU DO?

What is one way you can use your freedoms?

GLOSSARY

CONSTITUTION - a written record of the basic beliefs and laws of a country that states the powers and duties of the government and the rights of the people.

PROTECT – to guard someone or something from harm or danger.

RELIGION – a set of beliefs, values, and practices based on the teachings of a spiritual leader.

UNITED NATIONS – an international organization that helps countries around the world cooperate on international laws, human rights, and world peace.